Capture
the
Moment

Volume I

Why Journal

IS IT NECESSARY?

MULENGA CHANDA

Outskirts Press, Inc.
http://www.outskirtspress.com

ISBN: 978-1-4787-9311-3

PRINTED IN THE UNITED STATES OF AMERICA

Table of Contents

Chapter 1: Journaling.. 1

Chapter 2: Forms of Journaling 4

Chapter 3: Prompts for Journaling................................... 7

   1. Start Where You Are 7

   2. Create a Thinking Space....................................... 9

   3. Concentration and Focus 11

   4. Taking Time To Pray 13

   5. Personal Reflection 15

   6. Discipline and Timing 19

   7. Meditation 21

   8. Getting Deeper in Recording of Events 24

   9. Keep Your Jotter Handy 26

   10. Make Rest a Necessity 28

Chapter 4: Why Journal?.. 30

Chapter 5: Journaling Insights 31

1. Enrich Your Present from Your Past.................................... 31

2. A Point of Reflection 32

3. Write Your Way to a Great Future...................................... 33

4. Recording Past Events 34

Chapter 6: Avoid the Pitfalls of Journaling.................................... 35

1. Lack of Transparency.. 35

2. Procrastination... 35

3. Comparison Trap.. 36

4. Inappropriate Security.. 36

5. Be Realistic 37

6. Inappropriate Environment 38

7. Inaccessibility... 38

8. Indiscipline 39

9. Belief that Journaling Is the Ultimate Way to Enhance
    Your Achievements 40

10. Focusing Only on Religious Topics 40

11. Focusing on Personal Gain and Gratification 41

Conclusion- Journaling Enhances Success 42

Habakkuk 2:2 (KJV)
And the Lord answered me, and said,
Write the vision, and make it plain upon tables,
that he may run that readeth it.

Philippians 4:6 (KJV)
Be careful for nothing; but in everything by prayer and supplication
with thanksgiving let your requests be made known unto God.

My Personal Expectations from this Journal

_____
_____
_____
_____
_____
_____
_____
_____
_____
_____
_____
_____
_____
_____
_____
_____
_____

Acknowledgments

I happened to be at the famous Joyce Meyer conference in Missouri and spent a lot of time reflecting. I suddenly had the inclination to do a journal, and I prayed, "Lord, I would like to complete this journal before I leave the soil of Missouri." Thus this book was written on September 24, 2017,in St. Louis. I believe it will inspire you to greater heights.

I am a great believer in journaling and got the inspiration to write from my pastor's late wife, Pastor Ify Irukwu. She taught me to journal, and I embraced it. I would therefore like to honour her legacy for the great insight and wisdom she imparted to lot of people, but especially I appreciate the part she played in my life.

I am grateful to God for His unending love and mercies that are new every morning. I cannot express in words my growing love and desire for You, Lord, as you get sweeter. You never cease to amaze me as you unfold me before my eyes giving me the ability to do things I never imagined I could do.

To my precious husband, Nick, thank you for encouraging me and being there at all times to guide and support me. Your endless hours of prayer for me can never be appreciated enough.

To our three children Natasha, Neriah, and Seth-Joshua - you are lovely children. I know how much you have to sacrifice, having a twenty-four-hour working mum and dad, and still smile, are happy, content and loving. Thank you for the beautiful smiles, kisses, and hugs.

I would like to thank my pastors, Pastor Agu Irukwu, and his dear wife, Pastor Sola Irukwu, who have been of great support to my husband and myself. We appreciate your constant love and encouragement which gives me even greater confidence to keep moving forward.

I would like to thank my spiritual father, Pastor Cleddie Keith, of Cincinnati, Kentucky, for always being there and believing in me and Prophetess Francina Norman for the prophetic words that could have only come from the throne room of God, and all my friends around the world for your love, care and support.

I would especially like to thank my immediate family, whom I love and appreciate, and my extended family. Thank you for being there. I pray all goes well with you.

Last but not the least, I would like to thank my family at Revival Christian Church Enfield, London for your love and support.

Thank you!

Chapter 1: Journaling

Journaling is a helpful tool for people who would like to take special note of the different seasons in their life. Journaling is a journey that can be embraced as enhancing and bringing value to life or be unappreciated as not having much value. Well, I felt that way before and that I was wasting my time until I got to appreciate the words, thoughts, insights, and overall direction for my life being steered in the right way through journaling. I could not find any failure in journaling, only great gains. I found that even just going back to some memories I had written down in my journal was quite enlightening.

A journal, therefore, should be birthed from a personal perspective of how you feel by recording memories of past, present or future. The focus of journaling can be from different angles such as communing with God, having that dialogue and writing down what God is saying to you, be it in the form of prayers or meditation on scriptures. It is important to hear what God is saying to you. It's always good to reflect on God's providence and write it down.

In the same way, I realize that people are unique; they certainly can have their own way of journaling. I always say effective journaling can be done best in a format prescribed by the writer, whether it's writing in a traditional notebook or logging your thoughts onto a desktop, laptop computer or any other mobile device. In these modern times, there are special software programs that are so good at allowing for effective organization and the ability to access the journal anytime depending on internet provisions. It is important to note that the journal can be saved in various accessible formats. This is purely based on personal preference including what information and how much information to write and contain therein. Hence, there is no right or wrong way of journaling, rather just preferred styles. I suppose another important factor to take into consideration is the decision to keep a journal private or public which is up to the journal owner.

As human beings, we go through a lot of things that are worth writing down. Moreover, as a Christian, a journal can encompass different facets of our life, including the spiritual aspect. It's always good to look back and see what God has said to you in the past and build on it for the future. Writing causes people to revisit their own words, which they can reflect on and perhaps see things from a different perspective. For some, journaling could be as simple as keeping track of a day's events.

I personally find that the Christian life I lead is fast paced, and I literally have to keep up with myself to be able to write. The word journal is described as a way of keeping news and records of events in your life on a daily basis. I believe we can interchange journaling for the phrase keeping a diary of events. Journal writing is a journey that is achievable in many different ways, depending on the person's character, wishes and desires but especially the naturalness of how information resonates with them.

In the journey of journaling for a Christian, I believe the ultimate goal is to glorify God's name. As you look back on your personal journey, reviewing the words and insights God has used to carry you through, I am sure you can attest that it could only have been God. This is why it is so important to find an effective way of keeping the memories and reminding yourself of them. Looking back on my journals, sometime, I even wonder whether I am the one who wrote those words. As you follow through your journaling journey, your hopes are raised, your burdens are lifted, your faith is heightened, a refreshing arises, and your heart is filled with the confidence you've always had that with God, nothing is impossible (Luke 1:37) For with God nothing shall be impossible, and as Philippians 4:13 (KJV) says, "I can do all things through Christ which strengthens me."

Chapter 2:
Forms of Journaling

Some of the ways of journaling include the following:

1. Expressing thoughts, ideas and feelings that come to mind in a written form by either scripture meditation or personal reflection.

2. Drawing to express how you are feeling.

3. Writing past and present situations in life that are significant in some way.

4. For a Christian, dedicating time to hear from God and write down what He is saying, effectively getting direction from God.

5. Writing future plans and setting targets for your life.

6. Writing prayer requests and answers, and keeping a catalogue of these.

For effective journaling, it's always helpful to do this as a daily exercise because it's unbelievable how quickly events can be forgotten or misconstrued. This leads to information not written exactly the way it should be or situations not recorded as they actually happened. Always remember to include dates, as time passes very quickly.

Hence my recommendation is to try and write down the flow of events and thoughts right away using the most appropriate format, whether electronic or handwritten. I must say my preferred option is keeping a hard copy as it is secure and can be kept for years if stored appropriately and accessed when required. I have journals dating back ten years, and I am intrigued by them for many reasons, including how my handwriting has changed over time. Some of the information I read just makes me see how God has been faithful in my life countless times. Information is vital to your life so you should do everything possible to ensure it is kept clear, concise and secure.

Keeping a journal should not be a compelling matter. I believe it should be a delight with personal revelation and an understanding of the essence of journaling, which in turn encourages you to write with focus and intent. The process of journaling can naturally be an aspect of self motivation.

Journaling traditionally has been known simply as recording the past, but I would like to challenge every reader to practice journaling in order to be conversational with God. Christians can make the conscious effort to say, "I want to hear God," and set time aside to create a quality atmosphere where God speaks, and this is fully recorded.

As a Christian, I believe journaling creates an opportunity to develop a culture of talking to God. I envisage someone making it a regular practice to pick up his or her journal and wait to hear what God says to them. In my experience, the more I sit down to hear God, the more I get to hear Him talk and give me guidance.

Hearing from God and keeping track of what He says inevitably deepens your relationship with Him. The more time we afford God, the more God speaks to us. I believe time is always a great sacrifice that can be used to determine the seriousness of a relationship. Hearing from God and writing down the instructions and dictates of heaven concerning your life is a great strength that can be developed daily. For me, this is the height of journaling. I hear what God is saying to me, and I yield to His instructions and guidance in the way that best resonates with me.

Focused journaling based on a personal walk and relationship with God makes you answer to specific truths about yourself and where you are in a realistic manner. This also creates a sense of accountability because you know what God has said, when He said it, and what the significance of that word is. This creates a sense of initiative, making the effort to ensure that steps are made toward actualization of the dictates and promises of God. There should be a plan of taking step-by-step instructions in obedience to the spoken word of God. I must say that it is very clear when you meet someone who has embraced the precious journey of journaling and the place it holds in his or her life as the fruit of this labour are readily evident.

It is important to pay particular attention to journaling because it helps to describe who you really are, as you make your thoughts and ideas known in your own unique style which makes you understand yourself even better. I believe you get to see another side of yourself that you would have never seen otherwise. Organization, order, and self-actualization simultaneously follow journaling.

Chapter 3:
Prompts for Journaling

1. Start Where You Are

You might say, "I don't know where to start." My answer is to start where you are. You might just want to consider who you really are in Christ Jesus.

Write something positive about yourself or what the word of God says about you. Remember the good things you have done for your loved ones, and start writing down those positive thoughts and ideas as they freely flow. The more you think positively about yourself, the more you realize just how much potential you have. Having written down the positive words and attitudes about yourself, you instinctively develop the ability to be more creative, and that makes you think more positively. Write down as many positive ideas as you can think of.

Where I Am Starting

_____

_____

_____

_____

_____

_____

_____

_____

_____

_____

_____

_____

_____

_____

_____

_____

_____

_____

_____

_____

_____

_____

_____

_____

_____

_____

_____

_____

_____

2. Create a Thinking Space

It's always a great idea to have a designated "thinking space." This can be any place where you can focus. A place where you can easily adapt to hear God or to have your ideas, feelings, and thoughts jotted down. This can be anything from your room to a chair in the lounge, possibly when all the children are in bed if there are children in your life or it could be choosing a time when it's mostly quiet in your house or office environment. It goes without saying that the most appropriate writing environment enhances your ability to ensure concise writing, expressing your dreams, goals, and aspirations as the journey of journaling continues.

This is my thinking space, and I will do the following to make it work:

_____

_____

_____

_____

_____

_____

_____

_____

_____

_____

_____

_____

_____

_____

_____

_____

_____

_____

_____

_____

_____

_____

_____

_____

_____

_____

_____

_____

_____

_____

_____

3. Concentration and Focus

You need to make an effort to create time when you know you will pay special attention to writing and recording of the moment. Try making deliberate effort to take yourself away from the day-to-day mundane in order to do journaling. It's important to note that what people achieve without journaling cannot be compared to how much they will achieve having maximized their skill in journaling. If you don't give journaling focused time, I dare say another year will go by, and you won't even remember most of God's promises over your life.

Concentration and focus removes clutter from the mind and helps to hear God clearly thus achieving more dreams for the next level of your life.

Things I will do differently to enhance my concentration and focus:

_____

_____

_____

_____

_____

_____

_____

_____

_____

_____

_____

_____

_____

_____

_____

_____

_____

_____

_____

_____

_____

_____

_____

_____

_____

_____

_____

_____

_____

4. Taking Time To Pray

A lot of people underestimate the power of prayer. The Bible says in Philippians 4:13 (KJV),
"I can do all things through Christ which strengthens me." This is a clear indication so far that it is God who gives us the ability to do what we do. If and when you pray for God's guidance in what to write about, He will direct your path. It is therefore essential to pray because as you do so, you create the best avenue for God to speak to you in every area of your life and bring to your remembrance the things that are so pertinent for your well-being. Please pray for every area of your life, finances, health, ministry, work, friends, family, and education or business as the need may be and I can assure you that God will not be silent. Be sure to find out God's specific purpose for your life.

When you pray, God will unfold to you the different things He wants to draw to your attention. Always stop and ask God what to journal about. Remember to listen to what God is saying. Prayer should be a dialogue and not just you speaking.

Yes, capture the moments, but don't forget to ask God what He wants you to write down. The most important thing is to remember to accomplish God's will for your life!

I took time to pray, and God said the following regarding my health, finances, ministry, work, friends, family, and or education or business:

_____
_____
_____
_____
_____
_____
_____
_____
_____
_____
_____
_____
_____
_____
_____
_____
_____
_____
_____
_____
_____
_____
_____
_____
_____
_____
_____

5. Personal Reflection

Think about your life and how well you have managed so far in general. Then single out the different areas of your life individually, and identify where your major strengths and weaknesses are. In areas of weakness, reflect on how you can get stronger, and in areas of strength, think about how you can be strengthened. Think about what you will do to ensure you don't lose your strength. Seek guidance, ensure plans are in place on how your strengths will be maintained and how your weaknesses will be made stronger by for instance assessing your environment, paying attention to people you have surrounded yourself with even assessing the level of inspiration drawn from leaders and mentors where applicable. Pay attention to how much reading you are committed to and the value this brings to you. Think about all the different actions you do, why you do them, and what positive or negative influence they carry. Think about how you respond to people around you and whether this carries positive or negative feedback. Think about how you respond to situations and if God is at the centre of your responses. Thinking through all of the above gives you personal reflection, as does writing down insightful thoughts about who you really are, who you could be, and how you could do things differently to make a more positive impact that brings with it a sense of fulfilment and achievement. Personal reflection opens you up to new arenas in your life.

My Personal Reflections:

_____
_____
_____
_____
_____
_____
_____
_____
_____
_____
_____
_____
_____
_____

Building on my weaknesses;

_____
_____
_____
_____
_____
_____
_____
_____
_____
_____
_____
_____
_____
_____

Maintaining and building my strengths;

_____

_____

_____

_____

_____

_____

_____

_____

_____

_____

_____

_____

_____

_____

_____

_____

_____

_____

_____

_____

_____

_____

_____

_____

_____

_____

_____

_____

_____

_____

What I will do about my strengths and weaknesses;

_____
_____
_____
_____
_____
_____
_____
_____
_____
_____
_____
_____
_____
_____
_____
_____
_____
_____
_____
_____
_____
_____
_____
_____
_____
_____
_____
_____
_____
_____

6. Discipline and Timing

In journaling, discipline is a crucial focal point that brings about the intended outcomes. You might have the desire to journal, but without discipline it is highly unlikely that much will be achieved. Timing is so important, and you need to maximize this in journaling. You might like to make few considerations that will involve being able to look at your personal life and identify where most of your time is lost.

This will allow you to look inward and see how you can make adjustments.

I understand that you may be faced with a lot or personal requests from friends and family. Sometimes you might just need to have the ability to say, "I am sorry, but I can't help," rather than saying yes to everyone's request and failing to meet the demands of your promises.

I must say, being realistic will actually ensure your integrity is upheld and you will earn more regard for being honest.

This will certainly improve your skills in ensuring good time management enabling you to maintain discipline and timing.

I commit to the following disciplines to enhance my timing:

_____

_____

_____

_____

_____

_____

_____

_____

_____

_____

_____

_____

_____

_____

_____

_____

_____

_____

_____

_____

_____

_____

_____

_____

_____

_____

_____

_____

_____

7. Meditation

Looking back at my own life, the precious moments of journaling enhanced my ability to ponder God's word. It became a delight to wait for God and to hear what else He could show me through scripture. The Bible declares in Psalm 111:2, "Great are the works of the Lord; they are pondered by all who delight in them." Journaling helps us ponder God's word and relate the revelation received to God's sovereignty.

When you apply yourself to meditation of God's word and the scripture, the mind naturally tends to stray. It is important as you meditate not to allow personal thoughts to take over but to concentrate and focus on the scripture upon which you are meditating. "I will meditate on your precepts and fix my eyes on your ways" (Psalm119:15).

Take delight in the reading and study of God's word, but also hunger to hear what else God has to say by meditation of His word. The Bible says in Joshua 1:8, "This Book of the Law shall not depart from your mouth, but you shall meditate on it day and night, so that you may be careful to do according to all that is written in it. For then you will make your way prosperous, and then you will have good success."

It is important to simply meditate on God's word and wait for His leading and direction. If you stand in obedience to God's word and ask for the help of the Holy Spirit, He promises that He will make your ways prosperous.

Be sure to follow the instructions and guidance of the Holy Spirit applying them to your life; then you shall have success.

Hence, for me, the discipline of journaling enhances the ability of meditation.

Try meditation today by getting one of your favourite scriptures and writing it down. Then talk to God and ask Him to speak to your heart about this scripture. Write down and keep writing the more God reveals to you!

_____

_____

_____

_____

_____

_____

_____

_____

_____

_____

_____

_____

_____

_____

_____

_____

_____

_____

_____

_____

_____

_____

_____

_____

_____

_____

8. Getting Deeper in Recording of Events

It is such a pleasure to be able to journal from where you are at in your own personal life. Taking time to pray about different situations in your life and writing down what you feel God is saying is a great strength. Being realistic is essential.

Write about how you feel and what you believe God is saying to you.

You will find that the more open you are to God, the more He pours Himself onto you. God will fill up whatever time and space you give Him, so remember to give Him your all.

Being able to write about the different areas of your life and where you believe God is taking you creates a great foundation that you can continue building on as you Journal. As you write, always remember to stop and listen to what God is saying at every step of the way.

This is what God is saying to me:

_____

_____

_____

_____

_____

_____

_____

_____

_____

_____

_____

_____

_____

_____

_____

_____

_____

_____

_____

_____

_____

_____

_____

_____

_____

_____

_____

_____

_____

9. Keep Your Jotter Handy

It is often the case that God drops an idea in your heart, or you think of something, or someone says something that is important and you wish you could jot it down, but unfortunately you are unprepared and have no means of capturing the moment.

I believe their is need for focused planning with intent in order to be able to write those precious memories down. I believe that to purpose and say, "I will jot it down," would prompt you to ensure you have the most efficient and effective way of capturing your own moments. I'm sure you have heard of the famous saying that not planning anything is planning to fail.

It is a treasure to be able to record special moments in Your life and this being possible by being able to actually capture the special moments as they take place by writing them down. The best thing is to prepare and take note.

My personal recommendations for keeping my jotter handy:

10. Make Rest a Necessity

It is clear that when the body and mind are rested, there is a tendency to hear God more clearly. So please take time out of your usual busy schedule to rest.

From a place of rest, you tend to hear more instructions from God concerning your life. You are more inclined to yield to the spirit of God.

God will open your mind to many unthought-of treasures and give you fresh insight on what to do, and you will be able to make appropriate decisions for the way forward in your life.

The Bible says in Matthew 11:28 "Come to me, all who labour and are heavy laden, and I will give you rest." From a place of rest comes revelation.

I will do the following to ensure adequate rest:

_____

_____

_____

_____

_____

_____

_____

_____

_____

_____

_____

_____

_____

_____

_____

_____

_____

_____

_____

_____

_____

_____

_____

_____

_____

_____

_____

_____

_____

_____

_____

Chapter 4:
Why Journal?

It's important to take time to stop and write what you may be going through at different points of your life.

I believe journaling will help you and many others in the area of personal development. Journaling will also help you to create memories for significant experiences you have had over a period of time that you engage in journaling.

You will never know the time when you will need to get back to your journal and see the goodness of God over your life and consequently increase your faith. Journaling makes you appreciate the faithfulness of God over your life.

Let me emphasise that journaling is not compulsory but carries with it great benefits for anyone who would like to enjoy this journey of journaling.

Oftentimes journalling makes you stop to hear what God is saying concerning your present situation, either by Him talking to you personall, by His word or through reputable people.

As you apply yourself to His word, He will inspire you and show you what you ought to write. If you yield to God, you will certainly get inspiration from Him. You can also open the Bible and start journaling about your thoughts on scripture and then lead into your personal life and observations. The Bible is a timeless source of wisdom and spirituality that is helpful in all situations.

Chapter 5:
Journaling Insights

1. Enrich Your Present from Your Past

At times, every one of us faces so many challenges that we want to look back at past victories to encourage ourselves in the Lord. We say to ourselves, If God did that for me, I am sure He will do much more for me again. It's a question of faith. Our faith is built up because we have seen victories in our lives; therefore, we are encouraged when we look back at those victories, just as David said in

1 Samuel 17:33–36 (KJV):

> And Saul said to David, Thou art not able to go against this Philistine to fight with him: for thou art but a youth, and he a man of war from his youth. And David said unto Saul, Thy servant kept his father's sheep, and there came a lion, and a bear, and took a lamb out of the flock: And I went out after him, and smote him, and delivered it out of his mouth: and when he arose against me, I caught him by his beard, and smote him, and slew him. Thy servant slew both the lion and the bear: and this uncircumcised Philistine shall be as one of them, seeing he hath defied the armies of the living God.

Look at all the past victories and be thankful to God, telling Him you have confidence in Him.

This instantly builds your faith in God, and you are assured of the victory. Your faith in God's ability to give you a break through is followed by a sense of joy and fulfilment in God. God has a great future for you as long as we rest assured in Him.

2. A Point of Reflection

A journal is usually private, but sometimes you might want to share a few insights from it. The journal carries with it phenomenal ideas, and there maybe times you would like to refer to these great writings to encourage yourself or someone else. It always means a lot knowing that they are real, genuine, and personal. Many people will identify with these insights and have hope for themselves. The journal then becomes a place of discovery, not just for you but for other people as well, making it even more of a treasure. However, I must emphasize that this is purely a personal decision.

The more you write, the more you are able to think through your situation.

When attentive to God's voice, He gives you the ability to think carefully and even write about your thoughts and feelings.

As you write, you can get to a deeper place because I belivery writing carries with it the ability to intensify thoughts. As a human being, you can only remember so much, but the more you write, the more you are able to look back and develop what God has been speaking to you. Journaling enriches a person's path of life.

I love journaling because it oftentimes makes me stop and think about who I am in Christ Jesus and that my identity is rooted in Him. It is healthy to look inward at how you are doing and to remain positive in everything you do.

I think this is a good time to reflect on how you respond to situations and people around you, and especially yourself making various considerations as you journal.

God will keep enlightening you as you stay blended in Him.

3. Write Your Way to a Great Future

A lot of ideas start just as a thought. My advice to you is write it down. God will many times prompt you to write and may even give you scriptures that relate to your future situation. God will give you many promises, which you are likely to forget in just a few weeks.

Life is too fast, and we need to help ourselves by remembering that what God says to us is important and could be pivotal when making important decisions.

Journaling allows us to see our current state, where we are coming from and effecting where we are going. It will help us monitor our progress against the targets we may have set for ourselves. Journaling, therefore, enhances your personal development as you move to the next phase of your life.

In life you are faced with so many situations, and decisions have to be made. I believe taking a few minutes of focused effort to look at life more closely with a pen and paper or on a computer, whichever form you choose, will definitely guide you to a better future. Decisions will be well thought through before conclusions are made.

I believe you can sometimes use the journal to set goals and targets for the future and write down plans for how you intend to achieve them. The fact that you take time to write them down indicates you are making positive steps toward achieving these objectives.

Surrender your will by giving God all your plans. Tell God you surrender your entire life to Him and lay this at His feet. The more you let God in your life, the more He is magnified in you and through you.

4. Recording Past Events

Despite the many aspects to journaling, capturing the past is certainly one of the most clear-cut instincts along this journey.

In life, their are unique moments in which something significant happens or you receive a prophetic word and need to write it down so you don't miss it. It is rather very important to keep a catalogue of these moments so you can always look back at the great providence of God.

Looking back at what God has done in your life is a great way to acknowledge the grace of God over your life and to enhance your faith as you look back and acknowledge the faithfulness of God.

Recording the past will increase your faith and you can always point people in the direction of the great mercy of God and His ability to do what may seem impossible to achieve.

Chapter 6:
Avoid the Pitfalls
of Journaling

1. Lack of Transparency

The journal is yours, recording information accurately will allow for the best benefits and outcomes in your journaling.

It is imperative to write things down as they are. I believe there is a natural benefit in being realistic and genuine before God.

John 8:32
And you will know the truth, and the truth will set you free.

2. Procrastination

Not writing things down immediately will tamper with the accuracy of the information recorded. A lot can be forgotten or misconstrued. The danger of procrastination is that you may never even record that vital information. If you don't record, you can't look back to see how you have been victorious, as ultimately looking back at these victories increases your faith. It is necessary as a Christian to pay attention to what God says, thereby being alert spiritually. I am a strong believer that procrastination is a thief of time. Pay particular attention to details ensuring they are written down.

Proverbs 13:4
The soul of the sluggard craves and gets nothing, while the soul of the diligent is richly supplied.

3. Comparison Trap

The journal is yours and describes who you are and how you record information. It is therefore a unique document that is specific to you. Don't get caught trying to Journal the way someone else journals. Hence using a form of journaling that someone else treasures but does not appeal to you will not create adequate results that you intend to achieve. Remember, journaling is a personal walk, and so it is specific to you. You are unique and so everything about you must resonate well within your spirit.

2 Corinthians 10:12 (KJV)

For we dare not make ourselves of the number, or compare ourselves with some that commend themselves: but they measuring themselves by themselves, and comparing themselves among themselves, are not wise.

4. Inappropriate Security

It's necessary to point out that journals are treasures that take a lot to put together. They are precious pieces of work that pertain to you and will contain dreams, goals, and aspirations that need to be taken seriously.

Consideration needs to be made for the type of journal that will work best for you. It is important to for instance ask yourself the question, do I need a hard copy or a soft copy? If I go for a hard copy, where will be the best place to keep my journal securely? Will it be somewhere in my house or in the office?

On the other hand, you may choose to have an electronic journal. If this is the case, you need to consider how safe the information will be on your chosen device. How keen and diligent will you be in ensuring the safety of the data and that appropriate measures are in place, i.e. antivirus protection or safety code? Safety should be well thought through, whatever recording and storage options you choose. You need to pay particular attention to the storage of the journal to ensure information is never lost.

Psalm 16:8
I have set the Lord always before me; because he is at my right hand, I shall not be shaken.

5. Be Realistic

I believe when you decide to keep a journal, you need to assess your life and where you are at personally, and review your commitments and the different things happening in your life to be able to make a realistic assessment of the best times to do journaling. Journaling could be daily, weekly, spontaneous, or even combined.

It is essential to note that whatever schedules you decide on, they must not make you feel indebted; rather journaling should be something to look forward to.

It's also essential to realize that being realistic in journaling for a Christian is to have a dependency on God. Tell God exactly how you feel, and give Him all your aches, pains, joys, plans, and ideas that you may have concerning your life. I encourage you to be vulnerable before God as He is your father and always guiding you to move in your own God designed, unique and perfect divine plan for your life.

Proverbs 4:7
The beginning of wisdom is this: Get wisdom, and whatever you get, get insight.

6. Inappropriate Environment

Journaling needs to be done in the right environment for it to be effective. Having a conducive atmosphere will automatically enhance a positive approach which instinctly produces results. The right environment creates a great writing atmosphere that allows ideas to flow easily and enables you to hear God. If we take a seed, for example, and put it in an environment that is not quite right or conducive, the chances of it growing are slim if at all. In the same manner, if we don't create the right environment for focusing on achieving our goal of journaling, it's most likely not going to yield much fruit. I'm reminded of the parable of the sewer.

Matthew 13:8
Other seeds fell on good soil and produced grain, some a hundredfold, some sixty, some thirty.

Matthew 13:7
Other seeds fell among thorns, and the thorns grew up and choked them.

My prayer is that we will create the right environment for our journaling to yield a hundredfold return.

7. Inaccessibility

I have heard of people who choose the right form and style of journaling and get underway, but unfortunately they tend to forget their journal in the office or some other place. This creates gaps in journaling, which could lead to losing interest and eventually giving up.

Also, there are times when the journal cannot be accessed because it's in another part of the house, and you can't physically reach it because you are otherwise engaged. It's a good habit to keep a jotter handy so thoughts and ideas can be captured immediately and not forgotten. I have had many situations where God gives me ideas and I quickly access my phone and record the idea before I forget.

It is therefore important to keep the journal in a place where it is easily accessible to ensure those unique thoughts are captured. Ask the Lord for guidance.

Proverbs 3:5–6
Trust in the Lord with all your heart, and do not lean on your own understanding. In all your ways acknowledge him, and he will make straight your paths.

8. Indiscipline

One other pitfall we should be aware of is lack of consistency. It is important to realise that a lot of people make up their minds to journal and are excited about journaling because it would surely work for them. But they have not gained the courage to ensure consistency by continuous application of the discipline of writing. I must say, it can start off as mechanical, but with determination journaling quickly becomes a pattern that can be sustained. I know it can be inconveniencing initially but soon yields great results. Discipline can be applied where desired.

Hebrews 12:11
For the moment all discipline seems painful rather than pleasant, but later it yields the peaceful fruit of righteousness to those who have been trained by it.

9. Belief that Journaling Is the Ultimate Way to Enhance Your Achievements

It is a great pitfall to believe Christian journaling is the ultimate answer to personal progression and achievement. It is rather just one of the many avenues for personal development. There are many ways to enhance a personal walk, such as praying, Personal development courses, fasting, studying God's word, hearing from God and many more. All these avenues that bring divine revelation and insight into your life create advancement. Therefore, hearing God through various means and applying faith can help activate the potential that God has put in us. The key is to remain diligent in God, and He will use many other ways to enhance your life in addition to journaling.

Proverbs 21:5
The plans of the diligent lead surely to abundance, but everyone who is hasty comes only to poverty.

10. Focusing Only on Religious Topics

Unfortunately, some Christians tend to think journaling is only about religious topics. It is of paramount importance for every Christian to realize that they live in a conventional world and need to reflect on their personal situation in relation to all other important aspects of life, such as goals, interests, relationships, work, and desires. Committing every area of your life to God's hands enhances your ability to get better insight in all these different areas. You will be able to look at life aspects from a broader perspective and say, "What areas of my life need transformation?" It is important to commit all plans to God, and He will bring them to pass.

Proverbs 16:3
Commit your work to the Lord, and your plans will be established.

11. Focusing on Personal Gain and Gratification

We have to ensure that the foundation is right. Self-gratification does not enhance personal achievement or ascertain a great future in Christian journaling. There is only one person to whom we are mandated to attribute all the glory, honour, and adoration: the Lord Jesus Christ. It is not about you outside of God but rather about the abilities God has put inside of you for His own name's sake. It is therefore extremely important to always seek God's guidance and refer to God's written word.

Christian journaling is a path to spiritual breakthrough when it is faithfully committed to God while pursuing the unhindered, godly potential that God has deposited in us. The ultimate in Christian journaling is that your faith will increase, you will achieve more, and God will be glorified.

Matthew 5:16
In the same way, let your light shine before others, so that they may see your good works and give glory to your Father who is in heaven.

Conclusion-
Journaling Enhances Success

Journaling enhances success that lasts a lifetime. Success is not a form of wealth as some may interpret it, but rather it is doing God's will to accomplish the purpose for which you were created. There is an enhancement to life that comes with journaling because those who journal are focused on what they write about and can follow through their past and present achievements to forecast plans for their future, and as a result enhancing their plan and purpose of God over their lives.

This helps a person to make amends and make wiser decisions than he or she has done in the past. You can imagine how much this will help a Christian. Christian journaling was an eye opener for me. It helped me discover who I am, the potential God has placed inside of me, ability to keep record of achievements, being very realistic in goal setting but above all having a genuine relationship with God by regular communication and guidance of the Holy Spirit among many other reasons.

Journaling encompasses your overall well-being as you commit all the different areas of your life to God. This will certainly help you in living a life of integrity and leaving a great legacy that will inspire many more people to do Journaling as your achievements are clearly enhanced by the journey of journaling.

As you journal, you naturally embrace God's will in every area of your life and remain a great example. All you need to do is to commit the journey of journaling to God. Journaling naturally makes you enjoy and maintain your relationship with God.

Proverbs 16:3
Commit your work to the Lord, and your plans will be established.

 Lightning Source UK Ltd.
Milton Keynes UK
UKHW021944271218
334656UK00002B/17/P